AF326524

HOW TO LIVE LIKE A LATTER-DAY SAINT

How to Live Like a Latter-Day Saint

LEVI JONES

Balance

Contents

The Inward Life

Chapter 1

Prayer

Form
-If praying in private, kneel.
-If praying in public, fold your arms or clasp your hands.
-Uncover and bow your head.
-Fold your arms or clasp your hands.
-Pray audibly unless this would distract those around you.
-Address Heavenly Father.
-Thank Him for your blessings.
-Express your feelings.
-Ask Him for desired blessings.
-Close in the name of Jesus Christ and with the word "amen."

Content
-Pray with sincerity and the intent to follow God's will as it is revealed to you.
-Avoid unnecessary repetition and meaningless words and phrases.
-Confess your sins and ask for forgiveness.
-Ask for guidance in your decisions.
-Ask for strength to resist temptations.
-Ask for help in your life and work.
-Ask for blessings for your family, friends, and neighbors.
-Ask for protection.
-Express your love for God.
-Express gratitude for your blessings.
-Ask that God's will be done.
-Pause to listen for guidance after you finish your prayer.

Times
-Pray privately at least each morning and night.
-Pray with those in your home each morning and night.
-Pray before each meal to give thanks and ask for a blessing on the food.
-Pray as a group at the beginning and end of church meetings.
-Pray silently multiple times throughout the day.

2 Chr. 7:14
Ps. 55:17
Matt. 5:44
Matt. 6:5-7
Matt. 23:14
Luke 18:10-14
Luke 18:1
Acts 6:4
Col. 3:17
James 1:5-6
1 Ne. 15:11
3 Ne. 18:16
3 Ne. 18:20
3 Ne. 19:24
Alma 13:28
Alma 37:37
D&C 8:10
D&C 9:8
D&C 10:5
D&C 23:6
D&C 25:12
D&C 46:30
D&C 50:30
D&C 52:15
D&C 88:126
D&C 101:81
D&C 136:28
GP ch. 8 - Praying to Our Heavenly Father
GT - Prayer

Chapter 2

Sleep Habits

Maintain a consistent sleep schedule that allows you to get enough sleep.

Avoid oversleeping.

Go to bed early and get up early.

Prov. 6:9
Prov. 20:13
Eccl. 5:12
D&C 88:124
GT - Health
FSY - Your body is sacred

Chapter 3

Dress and Grooming

Maintain your clothing, hairstyle, and appearance in a way that honors your body as a sacred gift from God.

Avoid styles that draw inappropriate attention to your physical body.

Ex. 19:10
Deut. 22:5
1 Sam. 16:7
John 7:24
1 Cor. 3:16-17
2 Cor. 6:16
2 Cor. 7:1
2 Cor. 10:7
1 Tim. 2:9
Jacob 2:13
Alma 1:27
D&C 42:40
D&C 93:35
FSY - Your body is sacred

Chapter 4

Diet

Practice moderation in your eating.

Avoid wasting food.

Eat meat sparingly.

Eat a variety of fruits, vegetables, and grains.

Do not drink alcohol, coffee, or tea made from tea leaves.

Gen. 1:29
Gen. 2:9
Gen. 9:3
Judg. 13:13-14
Prov. 20:1
Prov. 23:20-21
Isa. 5:11
Isa. 5:22
Eph. 5:18
D&C 49:19
D&C 49:21
D&C 59:18-20
D&C 89:4-17
D&C 136:24
FSY - Your body is sacred
GP 29 - The Lord's Law of Health

Chapter 5

Addictive Substances

Do not use drugs except when necessary as medicine.

Do not use substances to produce an artificial effect that may be harmful to your body or mind.

Do not drink alcohol.

Do not use tobacco.

D&C 89:5-8
FSY - Your body is sacred
GP 29 - The Lord's Law of Health

Chapter 6

Entertainment and Media

Do not view or participate in anything that is excessively explicit in its depictions of sex or violence or that presents immoral behavior as acceptable.

Avoid pornography.

Do not use media in a way that invites contention or envy or that is otherwise harmful to your personal relationships.

Do not use media as a way to avoid doing other things you should be doing.

Phil. 4:8
Moro. 10:32
A of F 1:13
FSY - Walk in God's light
GT - Media

Chapter 7

Education and Learning

Obtain as much formal education as you reasonably can.

Seek opportunities for learning throughout your life.

Maintain a practice of reading books that will increase your wisdom and understanding of the world.

Prov. 1:5
Prov. 4:13
John 5:39
John 8:32
Col. 1:9-10
2 Ne. 9:28
2 Ne. 9:42
Alma 37:35
D&C 6:7
D&C 88:78
D&C 88:118
D&C 90:15
FSY - Truth will make you free
TTF - Education

Chapter 8

Scripture Study

Study the scriptures daily, both individually and with your family.

Deut. 6:6-7
Josh. 1:8
JS-M 1:37
2 Tim. 3:16
John 5:39
Rom. 15:4
2 Tim. 2:15
Rev. 1:3
1 Ne. 15:25
1 Ne. 19:24
2 Ne. 4:15
2 Ne. 31:20
2 Ne. 32:3
Mosiah 1:6-7
Alma 13:20
Alma 17:2
Alma 33:2
3 Ne. 10:14
D&C 1:37
D&C 11:22
D&C 21:4
D&C 26:1
D&C 33:16
D&C 84:57
D&C 93:53
FSY - Walk in God's light
GP ch. 10 - Scriptures

Chapter 9

Work

Perform honest work to provide for your family's needs.

Strive to care for extended family members who cannot meet their own needs.

Do your part to maintain your family's home.

Strive for financial self reliance but be willing to work with others.

Maintain a high standard for the work you do.

Gen. 3:19
Prov. 6:6
Prov. 14:23
Prov. 20:11
Eph. 4:28
1 Thes. 4:11
2 Thes. 3:8
2 Ne. 9:51
Mosiah 27:5
D&C 42:42
D&C 58:27
D&C 60:13
D&C 68:30
D&C 82:18
GP ch. 27 - Work and Personal Responsibility
FSY - Truth will make you free

Chapter 10

The Sabbath

If possible, rest from your regular work on Sundays.

Devote that day to worship, contemplation, and service to others.

Refrain from normal recreation on the sabbath.

If you cannot avoid regular work on the sabbath, strive to nevertheless maintain a spirit of worship in your heart.

Gen. 2:2
Ex. 16:23
Ex. 20:8-11
Deut. 5:12
Ex. 23:12
Ex. 31:13
Isa. 56:2
Isa. 58:13-14
Jer. 17:21-22
Matt. 12:10-13
Mark 2:27
Luke 13:11-17
Luke 14:2-6
John 5:16-17
John 7:23
D&C 59:9-13
D&C 68:29
GP - The Sabbath Day
TTF - Sabbath
FSY - Love God, love your neighbor

Chapter 11

Personal Finances

Avoid debt, with the exception of purchases for vital long-term needs such as a modest house and education.

Stick to a budget that allows you to live within your means while also donating to those who are in need.

Gradually build up savings to provide for your needs should financial difficulties arise.

Deut. 15:7-8
Mal. 3:10
Ps. 62:10
Prov. 11:28
Prov. 22:1
Prov. 28:27
Jer. 9:23
Matt 6:19-21
1 Tim. 5:8
Jacob 2:17-19
Alma 39:14
D&C 6:7
D&C 48:4
D&C 56:16
D&C 75:28
D&C 82:17-19
D&C 84:103
D&C 88:119
FG - Fulfilling Family Responsibilities
PENT

Chapter 12

Personal History

Keep a personal journal to record your experiences.

Maintain records of important events in the lives of your family members.

Mal. 3:16 (3 Ne. 24:16)

Moses 6:5

Moses 6:46

Abr. 1:31

TTF - Family History Work and Genealogy

FG - Fulfilling Family Responsibilities

The Outward Life

Chapter 13

Honesty

Be honest with God, with others, and with yourself.

Do not try to take more than you deserve.

Do not try to give less than you rightfully owe to others.

Ex. 20:16
Ex. 23:4
Ps. 24:3-4
Prov. 8:7
Prov. 12:22
Prov. 14:8
Prov. 14:25
Prov. 15:4
Prov. 16:13
Eccl. 5:5
Matt. 5:33-37
Rom. 12:17
Rom. 13:13
1 Cor. 3:18
2 Cor. 8:21
2 Cor. 13:7
Phil. 4:8
1 Thes. 4:11-12
1 Tim. 2:2
1 Pet. 2:12
1 Pet. 3:10
2 Ne. 31:13
Mosiah 4:28
Alma 41:14
3 Ne. 30:2
D&C 10:28
D&C 50:6
D&C 51:9
D&C 136:20, 25-26
GP - Honesty
FSY - Truth will make you free

Chapter 14

Language

Strive to edify in all of your communication.

Avoid crude language.

Do not be disrespectful or unduly casual when speaking about sacred things.

Use God's name with reverence.

Ex. 20:7
Lev. 24:16
Deut. 5:11
Ps. 34:13
Prov. 15:1-2, 7, 28
Prov. 21:23
Matt. 5:33-37
Matt. 12:36-37
Matt. 15:11
Mark 3:29
1 Cor. 15:33
James 1:26
James 3:2-13
Eph. 4:29
Col. 3:8
Col. 4:6
2 Ne. 26:32
Mosiah 4:30
D&C 63:61-62
D&C 108:7
D&C 136:21
TTF - Profanity
FSY - Love God, love your neighbor

Chapter 15

Sex and
Relationships

Do not have sex with anyone other than your spouse.

Avoid lustful thoughts about people other than your spouse.

Avoid arousing sexual feelings in anyone other than your spouse.

Do not use pornography or masturbate.

Gen. 2:24
Ex. 20:14
Lev. 18:6-20
Lev. 19:29
Lev. 20:10-21
Deut. 5:18
Deut. 22:20-30
Prov. 6:24-35
Prov. 12:4
Jer. 23:14
Jer. 29:23
Mal. 3:5
Matt. 5:27-28
Matt. 19:18
Rom. 1:26-27
Rom. 13:9
Gal. 5:16-17
Col. 3:5-6
2 Tim. 2:22
Titus 2:4-5
1 Nephi 22:23
3 Nephi 12:27-29
Jacob 2:27-28
Mosiah 13:22
Alma 23:3
Alma 30:10
Alma 39:3-5, 9
3 Nephi 12:32
Mormon 9:28
Moro. 9:9
D&C 42:22-26
D&C 42:74-77, 80

D&C 59:6
D&C 88:121
D&C 132:41-44
A of F 1:13
GP ch. 39 - The Law of Chastity
FSY - Your body is sacred

Chapter 16

Parenting

Ensure your children have the necessities of life.

Provide your children with an environment conducive to growth and improvement.

Teach your children true principles by which they can live good lives.

Show your children by your example how to live in harmony with the principles you teach them.

Deut. 4:9
Deut. 6:6-7
Deut. 11:18-19
Deut. 32:46
Ps. 78:2-8
Prov. 1:8
Prov. 13:24
Prov. 22:6
Prov. 23:13-14
Isa. 54:13
Eph. 6:2-4
Col. 3:20-21
1 Tim. 3:4-5
1 Tim. 5:8
1 Ne. 1:1
1 Ne. 8:37
2 Ne. 25:26
Jacob 3:10
Mosiah 4:14-15
Alma 56:47
3 Nephi 18:21
3 Nephi 22:13
D&C 55:4
D&C 68:25-28
D&C 75:28
D&C 83:4
D&C 93:40, 42-43
Moses 6:57-58
GP ch. 37 - Family Responsibilities
TFP

Chapter 17

Family History

Maintain a regular journal to record your experiences and important life events.

Research your family's history and share it with your children.

To the extent you can, ensure that your ancestors receive temple ordinances by proxy.

1 Chr. 9:1
Mal. 4:5-6
Matt. 16:19
1 Cor. 15:29
Heb. 11:40
1 Pet. 3:18-20
1 Pet. 4:6
1 Ne. 3:12
1 Ne. 5:14
Alma 37:3
Omni 1:18
D&C 110:12
D&C 124:39
D&C 128:15, 18, 24
D&C 132:46
D&C 138:47-48
Moses 6:8, 46
GP ch. 40 - Temple Work and Family History

Chapter 18

Meetings

Attend weekly sacrament meeting; stake, area, and general conferences; and other required meetings related to your church assignments.

Regularly participate in activities with your ward or branch.

Ex. 12:16
Lev. 23:3,7,27,35
Num. 29:1
Num. 28:25
Matt. 18:20
Acts 4:31
Acts 11:26
Heb. 10:25
Mosiah 18:25
3 Ne. 18:22
4 Ne. 1:12
Moro. 6:6
D&C 20:45, 61, 75
D&C 43:8
D&C 59:9
GP ch. 47 - Exaltation
GP ch. 23 - The Sacrament

Chapter 19

Missionary Work

Look for opportunities to share the gospel with others.

Prepare for and serve a full time mission shortly after you graduate from secondary school and when you retire from full time employment.

Isa. 49:6
Isa. 52:7
Isa. 61:1
Jer. 3:14
Jer. 16:16
Ezek. 3:17-21
Ezek. 34:11
Matt. 4:19
Matt. 5:19
Matt. 10:5-7
Matt. 24:14
Matt. 28:19
Mark 1:4
Mark 16:15-16
Luke 9:2
Luke 10:1
Luke 22:32
John 4:35-36
John 15:16
John 21:17
Acts 10:42
2 Tim. 4:2
Jacob 1:19
Mosiah 15:13-17
Mosiah 18:9
Alma 17:4
Alma 18:39
Alma 29:8
D&C 1:4-5
D&C 1:23
D&C 11:21
D&C 15:6

D&C 18:15
D&C 29:7
D&C 36:5
D&C 49:11-14
D&C 50:17
D&C 62:5
D&C 63:57
D&C 71:1
D&C 75:3-4
D&C 84:61
D&C 84:87
D&C 88:81
D&C 100:5-7
D&C 112:4-5
D&C 133:8
D&C 133:38
Moses 8:19
Abr. 2:9
GP ch. 33 - Missionary Work
TTF - Missionary Work

Chapter 20

Tithes and Offerings

Donate ten percent of your income to the Church.

Fast for two meals on the first Sunday of the month and donate the money you would have spent on those meals (if not more) to help the less fortunate.

Donate generously to other charitable causes as your circumstances allow.

Deut. 15:7-8
Lev. 27:30-31
Deut. 14:22
Mal. 3:8-12
Ps. 112:9
Prov. 3:9
Prov. 22:9
Prov. 28:27
Isa. 58:6-7
Matt. 5:42
Matt. 6:1
Matt. 19:21
Mark 12:41-44
Luke 11:41
Luke 12:33
Acts 20:35
Jacob 2:17
Alma 34:28
Mosiah 4:26
Mosiah 18:27
D&C 42:30-31
D&C 44:6
D&C 56:16
D&C 64:23
D&C 85:3
D&C 97:12
D&C 105:3
D&C 112:1
D&C 119:4
TTF - Tithing
GP ch. 32 - Tithes and Offerings

Chapter 21

Service

Look for opportunities to provide meaningful service.

Regularly visit, serve, and pray for the people to whom you are assigned as a ministering brother or sister.

When you serve others, do not seek or expect recognition or other rewards.

Matt. 7:12
Luke 22:26
James 1:27
1 Cor. 12:25
1 Jn. 3:18
Gal. 5:13
Mosiah 2:17
Mosiah 4:15
Alma 34:28
D&C 4:2
D&C 24:7
A of F 1:13
GP ch. 28 Service
GP ch. 32 Tithes and Offerings
FSY - Love God, love your neighbor

Chapter 22

Citizenship

Obey the laws of the country in which you live.

Take seriously your right and responsibility to be informed about and participate in the civil society of which you are a part.

If you have a role in selecting civic leaders, seek those who are well qualified and of upstanding moral character.

Ex. 22:28
Ps. 82:3
Prov. 24:21
Eccl. 8:2
Eccl. 10:20
Matt. 17:24-27
Matt. 22:15-21
Acts 23:5
Rom. 13:1
1 Tim. 2:1-2
1 Pet. 2:13,17
Titus 3:1
Mosiah 4:13
Alma 1:1
D&C 58:21
D&C 98:4-10
D&C 101:77
D&C 134:1-12
A of F 1:12
TTF - Civil Government and Law
GT - Citizenship

Charity in All Things

Though I speak with the tongues of men and of angels, and have not charity, I am become as sounding brass, or a tinkling cymbal.

And though I have the gift of prophecy, and understand all mysteries, and all knowledge; and though I have all faith, so that I could remove mountains, and have not charity, I am nothing.

And though I bestow all my goods to feed the poor, and though I give my body to be burned, and have not charity, it profiteth me nothing.

Charity suffereth long, and is kind; charity denvieth not; charity vaunteth not itself, is not puffed up,

Doth not behave itself unseemly, seeketh not her own, is not easily provoked, thinketh no evil;

Rejoiceth not in iniquity, but rejoiceth in the truth;

Beareth all things, believeth all things, hopeth all things, endureth all things.

Charity never faileth: but whether there be prophecies, they shall fail; whether there be tongues, they shall cease; whether there be knowledge, it shall vanish away.

For we know in part, and we prophesy in part.

But when that which is perfect is come, then that which is in part shall be done away.

When I was a child, I spake as a child, I understood as a child, I thought as a child: but when I became a man, I put away childish things.

For now we see through a glass, darkly; but then face to face: now I know in part; but then shall I know even as also I am known.

And now abideth faith, hope, charity, these three; but the greatest of these is charity.

1 Cor. 13

Abbreviations

A of F - Articles of Faith
Abr. - Abraham
Chr. - Chronicles
Col. - Colossians
Cor. - Corinthians
D&C - Doctrine and Covenants
Deut. - Deuteronomy
Eccl. - Ecclesiastes
Eph. - Ephesians
Ex. - Exodus
Ezek. - Ezekiel
FG - Family Guidebook
FSY - For the Strength of Youth
Gal. - Galatians
Gen. - Genesis
GP - Gospel Principles
GT - Gospel Topics
Heb. - Hebrews
Isa. - Isaiah
Jer. - Jeremiah
Jn. - John
Josh. - Joshua
Judg. - Judges
JS-M - Joseph Smith—Matthew
Lev. - Leviticus
Mal. - Malachi
Matt. - Matthew
Moro. - Moroni

Ne. - Nephi
Num. - Numbers
PENT - Prepare Every Needful Thing
Pet. - Peter
Phil. - Philippians
Prov. - Proverbs
Ps. - Psalms
Rev. - Revelation
Rom. - Romans
Thes. - Thessalonians
TFP - The Family: A Proclamation to the World
Tim. - Timothy
TTF - True to the Faith

www.ingramcontent.com/pod-product-compliance
Lightning Source LLC
Chambersburg PA
CBHW060635080726
47818CB00004B/153